PMS

When It's "That Time of the Month"

Amy Baker
with Daniel Wickert

New Growth Press

www.newgrowthpress.com

New Growth Press, Greensboro, NC 27404
www.newgrowthpress.com
Copyright © 2012 by Amy Baker and Daniel Wickert.

All rights reserved. No part of this publication may be reproduced, stored in a retrieval system, or transmitted in any form by any means, electronic, mechanical, photocopy, recording, or otherwise, without the prior permission of the publisher, except as provided by USA copyright law. Published 2012.

All Scripture quotations, unless otherwise indicated, are taken from the *Holy Bible,* New International Version®, NIV®. Copyright © 1973, 1978, 1984 by International Bible Society. Used by permission of Zondervan. All rights reserved.

Cover Design: Faceout Books, faceout.com
Typesetting: Lisa Parnell, lparnell.com

ISBN 13: 978-1-938267-82-6
ISBN 13: 978-1-938267-23-9 (eBook)

Library of Congress Cataloging-in-Publication Data
Baker, Amy
 PMS : when it's "that time of the month" / Amy Baker with Daniel Wickert.
   p. cm.
 Includes bibliographical references and index.
 ISBN 13: 978-1-938267-82-6 (alk. paper)
 1. Christian women—Religious life. 2. Premenstrual syndrome—Religious aspects—Christianity. I. Title.
 BV4527.B28   2012
 248.8'6198172—dc23

2012026547

Printed in Canada

19 18 17 16 15 14 13 12   1 2 3 4 5

After snapping at her children for the third time in thirty minutes, Noel flees to her bedroom in tears. She hates this time of the month, five days before her period. Normally patient and self-controlled, Noel knows she'll be tired and irritable as she battles premenstrual syndrome (PMS). She knows that she'll be unreasonable with her husband and sharp with her children. And she knows that the whole thing will repeat itself next month—and the month after that.

Michelle doesn't tense up like Noel when she experiences PMS. Instead, she feels unmotivated. She doesn't want to get out of bed, and she drags herself around feeling depressed. Her friend Tori frequently experiences symptoms like headaches and bloating when her PMS kicks in. But for Tori, it's the unpredictable crying that's the hardest. Bursting into tears at work with little or no provocation has been very embarrassing.

No matter what their symptoms, all three women know that they will experience some relief when their periods start, but they also know that the cycle will repeat itself each month in the days leading up to their periods. It's discouraging and frustrating, especially when the only true relief seems to be years away with menopause.

If you're reading this booklet, chances are that you too struggle with PMS. Perhaps you've noticed mood swings, joint or muscle pain, weight gain due to fluid retention, acne flare-ups, and constipation or diarrhea in the days before your period. Perhaps fatigue, irritability, bloating, tension, breast tenderness, food cravings, forgetfulness, and headaches all make you want to cry. And you do cry—easily. PMS is a time of physical and emotional weakness.

PMS doesn't manifest itself in every woman in the exact same way, so your experience with PMS may be different from the experiences of other women you know. Some women don't seem to experience PMS symptoms at all. Additionally, for those who do experience PMS, the physical and emotional symptoms may be intense during some months but only slightly noticeable in other months.

Nevertheless, whatever power PMS seems to hold over your mood, thinking, emotions, body, appetite, and temper, it is not as powerful as Christ. Jesus is stronger than anything else in this world. His death and resurrection proves that (Colossians 2:10, 15). That means that PMS is not more powerful than God! That's a reason to turn to him in trust and faith and ask for his help. When you turn to God, he *will* help you. Our loving God wants *all* of your life to be changed

Amy Baker with Daniel Wickert

and transformed by his Spirit, and that includes the times you may struggle with PMS.

God wants to use the physical and emotional weakness you experience with PMS to lead you to rely on his power. As his dearly loved child, his heir who will share Christ's inheritance, God's great power is available to help you live in freedom and peace rather than guilt and frustration. What feels like an ailment that interferes with your life each month can become a means to grow in faith and faithfulness (1 Peter 1:6–7). God wants you to become like Jesus, and he uses everything in your life—even your PMS to accomplish this purpose.

Ask and Keep Asking

God wants to help you. When you find yourself tested each month with PMS symptoms, bring your feelings to God. He says that you can cast *all* your cares on him, so this is neither too big nor too small to take to him (1 Peter 5:7).

The Psalms record numerous occasions when people cried out to God and cast their cares on him. Psalm 31 is one example, but you can see the same pattern in many other psalms. Let's look at how the psalmist brought his struggle to God in Psalm 31 and identify a pattern that you can use to cast your cares on God.

1. *Call out to God.* Here's what the psalmist said: "Turn your ear to me, come quickly to my rescue; be my rock of refuge, a strong fortress to save me" (Psalm 31:2).
2. *Tell God about the trouble.* Describe it. The psalmist tells God that his enemies had a trap set for him (v. 4).
3. *Express trust in God.* The psalmist put it this way: "Into your hands I commit my spirit" (v. 5).
4. *Praise God for his love and care.* The psalmist worshiped, exclaiming, "I will be glad and rejoice in your love, for you saw my affliction and knew the anguish of my soul. You have not handed me over to the enemy but have set my feet in a spacious place" (vv. 7–8).

Yet Psalm 31 doesn't end there. This is a bit surprising, since you would think that once the psalmist has been rescued, the psalm would end. But in verse 9 the psalmist cries out again: "Be merciful to me, O LORD, for I am in distress; my eyes grow weak with sorrow, my soul and my body with grief." Although he has been rescued once already, he is again in need. God has come to his rescue once, but now the psalmist is struggling and asking for help again (perhaps for help with the same trial). The psalmist follows the same pattern as before.

1. He calls out (v. 9).
2. He tells God about the troubles (v. 10).
3. He expresses trust (vv. 14–15).
4. He worships and praises God (vv. 19–22).

The psalm ends with this encouragement to everyone who wants to cry out to God: "Be strong and take heart, all you who hope in the LORD" (Psalm 31:24).

So take heart and bring your struggle to God. Like the psalmist, you may need to repeat the process (and repeat and repeat and repeat). You may call out, express trust, experience God's grace to respond righteously and then three minutes later find that you need to cry out again. You can know that God's grace will be there for you every time.

God wants to pour out his grace on you (Ephesians 2:7). So take heart and ask for help, expecting that God has great goodness stored up for you. Cry out to God whenever you face the urge to sin or the temptation to give in. Keep on asking, and let the Lord preserve you.

"My Sins Have Overtaken Me"

PMS causes us to experience physical and emotional weakness, and one thing we certainly see in the middle of weakness is the temptation to sin. Jesus wants to help us at that point. He knows that PMS makes it hard (if not impossible) to avoid sinning by the use of willpower alone. But that's a good thing! We no longer have the illusion that we can solve our problems by our own efforts. Instead, in our weakness, we can learn like the psalmist to go to God in honest confession.

In Psalm 40:12, the psalmist moans that his sins have overtaken him and he cannot see. As we struggle with snapping angrily at those around us or slipping into self-pity, the strategies we often use to keep these sins at bay become useless and ineffective. Our sins overtake us.

The rest of the month, without the pressure of PMS, we may find that the desire for a good reputation or the approval of others, the ambition to be a good wife and mother, or any number of other desires are sometimes enough to keep us from responding to others irritably or slipping into depression. But those desires often aren't strong enough when we are battling PMS.

PMS often seems to override a desire for a good reputation or the approval of others. It often seems to undercut our ambition to be a great wife and mother. While at other times of the month these desires and ambitions may help us control irritability, moderate moodiness, and power through fatigue, God doesn't want these desires to become what we worship. God doesn't want his glory to be given to another (Isaiah 48:11), so he refines us by allowing us to experience difficult things.

When you experience PMS, your willpower is weak. That is humbling! But when you are in that place, all you have to do is ask and Jesus comes as your rescuer. When you are weak, his grace is so welcome. Because you can't help yourself or change yourself you have to depend on Jesus. Then you will find that his power is made perfect in your weakness (2 Corinthians 12:9). Now you see that his power is awesome. Now his grace seems especially sweet.

Month after month as you turn to God in dependent trust and faith, waiting patiently for him, you come to realize that any patience, gentleness, or goodness you display is all because of his grace in your life. It's *his* grace that enables you to gently cuddle your children rather than snap at them. It's *his* grace that enables you to respect your husband rather than be a shrew. It's *his* grace that enables you to cooperate with your colleagues rather than gossip about their shortcomings.

As you begin to see that every positive character quality you possess is an outpouring of his grace, your desire to worship increases. Other desires grow weaker and lose their enslaving power. Your confidence in God grows and you step forward in faith, looking eagerly toward deeper and deeper demonstrations of his grace. His grace is not only sufficient on days when you're *not* battling with PMS; it is sufficient when PMS is raging. As you understand that it is his grace that enables you to respond patiently when you *aren't* experiencing PMS, you look forward to deeper grace to respond patiently *with* PMS. You no longer try to make it through PMS on willpower; instead you cry out to God. Now you say to yourself, "PMS is not an excuse to sin; it is an opportunity to know God's grace in deeper ways." At the end of the refining process you find that God has equipped you to echo Isaiah 40:31, "[T]hose who hope in the LORD will renew their strength. They will soar on wings like eagles; they will run and not grow weary, they will walk and not be faint."

Plan Like You Know It's Coming

When you experience PMS, life will be harder. Yet God gives his grace to help you. Like any good event organizer who prepares for possible mishaps, you should use God's grace to prepare in advance for the difficulties you typically face.

1. Equip Your Body

As believers, we are to offer our bodies as a living sacrifice to him (Romans 12:1), ready for his use. When you anticipate PMS, equipping your body may include exercising; taking vitamins; eating nutritiously; limiting caffeine, sugar, and salt that can aggravate PMS symptoms; and getting a proper amount of sleep. Equip your body to serve God well.

Tori has learned that she must curb her intake of potato chips and french fries to minimize some of her PMS symptoms. Although she loves salty snacks, she has become convinced that she shouldn't call out to God for help and then refuse to make changes in her diet. Instead, when she's drawn to salty snacks, she has begun writing notes of encouragement to others. This keeps her mind and hands occupied so that she won't automatically reach for something salty.

Equipping your body may also include getting counsel from your doctor regarding treatments for PMS.

As you equip your body, remind yourself that these practices are not your savior. Your hope is in God, not the elimination of PMS symptoms. If God chooses to use your efforts to reduce your symptoms, you can praise him for his grace. But if your PMS symptoms are not relieved, you can have confidence that God still has a good plan for you. He can still help you grow in grace and glorify him if your PMS symptoms persist, and perhaps he has something specific to teach you. Trust that if God chooses not to take your PMS symptoms away, it is because he has something superior in store for you. You can still praise him—even though you will probably need to cry out simultaneously.

2. Examine Your Schedule and Commitments

Because you know that life can be more stressful when you experience PMS symptoms, arrange your calendar so that tasks that can potentially overwhelm you are not scheduled during that time. For example, you may decide that balancing your checkbook is not something you should attempt when you are fighting PMS. Forgetfulness, poor concentration, and irritability aren't generally helpful in reconciling one's checkbook! Plan instead to tackle that chore earlier in the month. Guard against procrastinating such tasks so that the pressures of having them hang over your head will not intensify your symptoms.

Additionally, as God allows, try to keep your calendar as free as possible during your PMS days. Try to schedule activities on days when you know you will have more energy.

Again, don't depend on these measures as if they are your savior, as if they are the only things you can count on to keep you from behaving badly during this time of the month. You will know that you have begun to see them as your savior if you begin *insisting* that you can't fulfill responsibilities or schedule extra activities when you are experiencing PMS. You will know that you have begun to see them as your savior when you become annoyed or depressed when your schedule gets rearranged, or when you no longer thank God for his grace, which allows you to moderate your schedule.

Christ is your Savior! He will give you the grace you need when things don't work out as you have planned.

3. Pray and Seek God's Help before Your PMS Kicks in Each Month

Jesus always prayed before entering into intensive times of ministry or suffering and he encouraged us to do the same. Noel and her husband decided to spend special prayer times together before and during her struggle with PMS. During these times Noel asked that they pray for the following:

- That God would alleviate Noel's symptoms if it is his will.
- That Noel would submit to God's will even if he doesn't ease her symptoms.
- That Noel would not use PMS as an excuse to sin.
- That God would help Noel rely on his grace to be kind and patient with others even when she does not feel like it.
- That Noel would display God's glory in the midst of her PMS.

- That God would use Noel's PMS to develop the fruit of the Spirit in her life (Galatians 5:22-23).
- That Noel would not dishonor her Savior during the hard days.
- That God would give Noel grace to praise him in the midst of her PMS.
- That God would also show grace to other women who struggle with PMS.

4. Equip Your Mind

Saturate yourself in Scripture passages that will strengthen you. This will keep you from sinning when you are under intense pressure (Psalm 119:11).

Michelle has found it helpful to write key verses on note cards to carry with her. She has also posted verses where she'll see them often—on her bathroom mirror, her computer monitor, her fridge, and next to her favorite chair. You may also find this helpful.

Following is a long list of Scripture passages that might help you. Why not pick one you really like, write it on a note card, and review it a few times each day? If you'll simply pull it out and review it once or twice a day for a week, you'll probably find that you know it as well as if you had memorized it.

- Remember that Psalm 31 gives a pattern for asking for God's help, encouraging you to be strong as you hope in the Lord.

    Psalm 31:24: "Be strong and take heart, all you who hope in the LORD."
- Remind yourself that God won't let you go through deep waters alone, nor will he allow you to be pulled under and swept away.

    Isaiah 43:2: "When you pass through the waters, I will be with you; and when you pass through the rivers, they will not sweep over you. When you walk through the fire, you will not be burned; the flames will not set you ablaze."
- Remember that God is giving you grace. He'll give you all you need.

    2 Corinthians 9:8: "And God is able to make all grace abound to you, so that in all things at all times, having all that you need, you will abound in every good work."
- Remind yourself that God is using PMS for your good—to make you like Christ.

    Romans 8:28-29: "And we know that in all things God works for the good of those who love him, who have been called according to his purpose. For those God foreknew he also predestined to be conformed to the likeness of his Son, that he might be the firstborn among many brothers."

- Remember, we are more than our hormones, and our hormones don't get to be the boss!

    Psalm 73:26: "My flesh and my heart may fail, but God is the strength of my heart and my portion forever."

- Remind yourself that God made you a woman and we know his plans are good.

    Psalm 139:13: "For you created my inmost being; you knit me together in my mother's womb."

- Remember that PMS cannot separate you from Christ and his love.

    Romans 8:35, 37–39: "Who shall separate us from the love of Christ? Shall trouble or hardship or persecution or famine or nakedness or danger or sword? . . . No, in all these things we are more than conquerors through him who loved us. For I am convinced that neither death nor life, neither angels nor demons, neither the present nor the future, nor any powers, neither height nor depth, nor anything else in all creation, will be able to separate us from the love of God that is in Christ Jesus our Lord."

5. Review Your Source of Hope

Will your hope be destroyed if you experience the symptoms of PMS even when you've asked God to remove them? Put your hope in God, not the removal of your symptoms. Entrust yourself to the Father: know that if he loved you so much that he didn't spare his Son, he'll graciously give you good things now (Romans 8:31-32). He'll take what seems like a curse and turn it into an opportunity to become a mirror image of Christ (Romans 8:29). Imagine being able to look into the mirror of your soul and see Christ reflected there. Truly, those who hope in God will never be disappointed (Isaiah 49:23).

When PMS Kicks In

If God chooses not to remove your PMS symptoms, you can still be joyful in hope, patient in affliction, and faithful in prayer (Romans 12:12). These six suggestions may help you.

1. *Remind yourself that God goes with you* through deep waters—and he holds them back so that they cannot sweep over you. He did this for Israel; he can do it for you (Isaiah 43:2). Thus, no matter how great the temptation to sin, it will never be more than God's grace will enable you to handle. He is holding

back anything that might truly overwhelm you, so remind yourself that you are not in over your head if you are relying on him. You can handle this when your powerful Savior is holding you by your right hand and denying the waters permission to pull you under and sweep you away.

Michelle has relied on this promise as she has disciplined herself to fulfill her responsibilities rather than retreating to her bedroom. She has prepared a "thank list" to help her focus on God's marvelous gifts to her rather than focusing on how difficult things are right now.

2. *Call out to God repeatedly.* Use the four-step pattern we talked about earlier. End each prayer with an expression of trust and confidence in God.
3. *Ask those closest to you to pray for you* and to remind you of God's truth.
4. *Refuse to permit PMS to be your excuse to sin.* Remind yourself of the way God has met your need with his grace in the past. When you are tempted, remind yourself that God's grace is more than enough to meet your need now (2 Corinthians 12:9).

5. *Continue to strengthen your body.* Take a walk, drink water instead of soda, schedule a nap, use pepper instead of salt—you get the picture.
6. *Humbly admit to your family that you are weak.* Ask if they will show you special grace in your time of need and help ease your load. (This means going without any expectations or demands which obligate your family. It's not humble if you *demand* that they show you grace!) God gives grace to the humble and he may use your family as his instruments of grace. God will also give you grace and strength to respond well even if your family doesn't ease your load.

Noel has been blessed with a family who serves her during these times by taking over the grocery shopping and meal preparation. On the rare occasions when they haven't, Noel has realized that God has given her extra grace. She has actually been cheerful about showing her family love as she shops and cooks.

When You Fail

When you fail, call it sin and run to God for mercy and forgiveness. When you ask God's forgiveness, he will remove your sin as far is the east is from the west (Psalm 103:12). God won't leave you in the pit into which you have fallen; he will rescue you. Not only will he pull you out, he will crown you with love and compassion (Psalm 103:4). In exchange for a pit you get a crown—what a marvelous demonstration of God's grace!

As you rejoice in his compassion, evaluate the factors that contributed to your fall so that you can be better prepared to fight temptation next time. It might be helpful to ask yourself questions such as the following:

- What did I want when I gave in to temptation?
- Can I identify a desire that ruled me?
- Did I believe that my PMS justified responding sinfully?
- Did my responses reflect the grace God has shown to me?
- Did I act as if God's resources and grace were not enough to help me handle temptation in a way that pleased him?
- What was I "worshiping" on that occasion? Was it a desire for peace, a desire to be left alone, a desire not to have PMS?

- Were my defenses weak against temptation because I've been neglecting my relationship with God?

Use your answers to prepare better for the future. If you have difficulty coming up with a plan, ask an older woman in your church, a wise and godly friend, or a biblical counselor to help you.

In addition to asking God's forgiveness, it would be good to humbly admit your failure and seek forgiveness from any others you have wronged. Sin breaks relationships. If you have given in to temptation, most likely others have been wounded. Seeking their forgiveness gives you an opportunity to restore your relationship. Asking forgiveness means 1) going to the person you have sinned against, 2) admitting specifically that what you said or did was wrong and why it was wrong, 3) expressing sorrow for the hurt you have caused, 4) explaining how you plan to change, and 5) asking the person to forgive you.

The Bible tells us that if we're genuinely sorry, others should be able to see evidence of this. They should be able to see the fruit of our repentance. Ask God for opportunities to exhibit this fruit to those you have hurt. Perhaps this would involve a special dinner for your husband, extra cuddling with your children, or building up your colleagues to others.

Finally, be strong and take heart. As we put our hope in the Lord, we'll find that PMS is no longer our excuse to sin. Instead, it's an opportunity to reflect our Savior's presence and work within us!

Simple, Quick, Biblical

Advice on Complicated Counseling Issues
for Pastors, Counselors, and Individuals

MINIBOOK
CATEGORIES

- Personal Change
- Marriage & Parenting
- Medical & Psychiatric Issues
- Women's Issues
- Singles
- Military

USE YOURSELF | GIVE TO A FRIEND | DISPLAY IN YOUR CHURCH OR MINISTRY

New Growth Press

Go to **www.newgrowthpress.com** or call **336.378.7775** to purchase individual minibooks or the entire collection. Durable acrylic display stands are also available to house the minibook collection.